Presented to:

_____

By:

_____

On the Occasion of:

_____

Date:

_____

THE WAY OF
$\mathcal{E}$XCELLENCE
FAITH

THE WAY OF
EXCELLENCE

FAITH

RAY PRITCHARD

MOODY PRESS
CHICAGO

Editorial Services: Julie-Allyson Ieron, Joy Media

Design: Ragont Design

ISBN: 0-8024-3177-1

1 3 5 7 9 10 8 6 4 2

Printed in the United States of America

For Joshua

Your faith has made you strong.

"Have I not commanded you? Be strong and courageous. Do not be terrified; do not be discouraged, for the Lord your God will be with you wherever you go."

JOSHUA 1:9

CONTENTS

Welcome to
the Journey of Faith

A friend said that for years she has been praying for a certain thing from God. It is a righteous and even noble request, but so far God has not seen fit to answer her prayer. As she prayed for patience, she realized that for a long time she was not ready to receive the answer. She came to the conclusion it was good that God had not answered her request.

Sometimes answers to our prayers are delayed because we need to grow deeper before God can say yes. That means trusting that God knows best and His timing is perfect. Sometimes it is better for God to say no to a legitimate prayer request so He might say yes to something better for us. Yet we don't usually see things in this perspective until much later—months or years down the road.

A young man entered a monastery where the schedule consisted of worship and contemplative prayer around the clock. How do you fight off boredom in such an atmosphere? He said some days boredom could become a problem because he was doing the same thing over and over. It could seem as if the road were leading nowhere. But there were moments, he said, when the clouds lifted, and he realized that the path he had been traveling was a winding road with many switchbacks as it climbed

toward the summit. In those moments of reve-
lation, he could look down and see how far he
had come.

Just like this man, you and I aren't to the top
of our uphill roads yet, but we've traveled a
long way from our starting points. Some of our
prayers are answered immediately, so we will
not despair; others are answered later, when we
are ready to receive them; some are never answered for reasons that lie hidden in the heart
of God. Meanwhile, we follow the winding
road, climbing toward the distant peak that
beckons us onward.

This book is about the faith that keeps moving
forward despite difficulties and delays. In the
next few pages we're going to talk about an-
swering God's call, taking tiny steps in a new

direction, having the courage to walk on water, obeying when it isn't easy, and passing our faith along to our children and grandchildren.

Faith is a journey that leads along a winding road that ends in heaven. The only thing God asks is that we take the next step and trust Him with everything else. If you'd like some practical help for the journey, turn the page, and we'll get started.

When God Calls

Hebrews 11:8

By faith Abraham, when called to go to a place he would later receive as his inheritance, obeyed and went, even though he did not know where he was going.

L et's imagine a dialogue between a middle-aged man named Abraham and God:

"Abraham, this is God speaking. I want you to leave everything and go to the land I will show you."

"Where's that?"

"If I told you, you wouldn't believe Me."

"Try me."

"It's one thousand miles from here in a place called Canaan."

"Never heard of it."

"I know, and guess what else?"

"What?"

"I'm going to make you the father of a great nation."

"That's impossible. I don't have any children."

"Don't worry."

"What do you mean, don't worry?"

"Just trust Me."

"Let me see if I've got this straight. You want me to leave everything, travel across the desert to someplace I've never heard of, and become the father of a great nation."

"Right."

"Is this some kind of joke?"

"No."

"What am I supposed to tell my wife?"

"That's your problem."

We can't understand what Abraham did until we ponder the last phrase of Hebrews 11:8, "By faith Abraham, when called to go to a place he would later receive as his inheritance, obeyed and went, *even though he did not know where he was going*" (italics added). He left Ur of the Chaldees because God called him, and in his leaving he left behind all he had known, all that was familiar. He left it all for an unknown future. How many of us would be willing to do that?

That's how it is in the life of faith. Many times you will be called to step out for God, and you will be precisely where Abraham was—believing God, but not knowing what the future holds.

When I think of that principle, my mind goes back to a conversation I had with Dan and Linda a few years ago. After a lifetime in the Chicago area, they were moving to Memphis, Tennessee. To say the move seemed incredible would be an understatement.

Around a campfire one night I had a long talk with Linda about her struggles with leaving the familiar surroundings of Chicago. Moving to Memphis for her was like going to a foreign country. The decision was more difficult because her husband had no contacts in Memphis, no promise of a job, no reason to move there at all, really.

※

*E*xcept one. Their close friends Len and Roberta had already moved to Memphis where Len had taken a new job. That played into the decision, but the rest of it made little sense. Beside the campfire Linda told me she had finally decided to go, and she was trusting God to work out the details. So they went. The first year in Memphis proved difficult. There was the culture shock, the impact of moving from a huge metropolitan area to a smaller city, the challenge of making new friends, getting the kids settled in school, finding a new church, and on top of that, Dan didn't have much work for a long time.

In the intervening years many things have happened, some of them difficult, indeed. Len developed cancer and died shortly after surgery. There were other challenges as Dan and Linda's children grew up, graduated from high school, and began to make

their own decisions about the future. Not long ago I received an e-mail from Linda in which she looked back over the last seven years. Nothing had gone as they had expected. If they had a "plan" when they moved to Memphis, it had been tossed out the window a long time ago.

❧

> Many times you will be called to step out for God, and you will be precisely where Abraham was—believing God, but not knowing what the future holds.

❧

For a while they had wanted to move back to Chicago, but that had never worked out. Linda commented that she and Dan can clearly see God's hand in everything that has happened to them. They have grown closer together, and their family is stronger than before. Clearly, God moved them from Chicago to Memphis for reasons that only now are becoming apparent. Their part was to obey, and so they went, knowing where they were going but not knowing why.

That story poignantly illustrates a central truth about the life of faith: You rarely see the big picture in advance. Even if you think you see it, you don't. When God calls, He doesn't always explain Himself. He tells you just enough to get you moving in the right direction. The rest is up to Him.

It is at this point that Abraham's greatness is clearest. God called, and he obeyed. Hebrews 11:8 says he "obeyed and went."

He may have doubted, *but he went*.

He may have argued, *but he went*.

He may have wondered, *but he went*.

When God calls, the only proper response is to obey and go.

A bus company once sought customers by inviting people to buy a ticket, get on board, and "leave the driving to us." That's not a bad motto for the life of faith. When God calls, move out by faith, and leave the driving to Him.

God of Abraham,
Save me from the folly
of asking so many
questions that I end up
using my questions as
an excuse not to obey Your
call. Give me faith to
obey even when I don't
understand why. Amen

If you had been Abraham, how would you have responded to God's call?

Have you ever had to make a major step of faith? What happened and what did you learn from that experience?

In what area of your life is God calling you to move forward by faith?

Tiny Steps

1 John 1:7

But if we walk in the light, as he is in the light, we

have fellowship with one another, and the blood

of Jesus, his Son, purifies us from all sin.

All of us are faced with thousands of small choices every day; each one moves us in one direction or another. In a sense, each small decision is a temptation, a testing, a moment when we decide whether we will walk in the light of God or go back to the darkness. Either you give in or you stand your ground. Each time you give in—even a little bit—you grow weaker; each time you resist— even a little bit—you grow stronger.

We only make progress when we walk in the right direction. To use the words of 1 John 1:7, we must actively choose on a moment-by-moment basis to "walk in the light."

A friend came to see me with news that after many years of struggle she had finally turned the corner in her battle against a debilitating addiction. I shared with her an illustration that has been helpful to me: Every day we make thousands of decisions—what to wear, which way to drive to work, when to go to lunch, which phone call to return first. Each decision is either a step into the darkness or a step into the light. I told my friend that each day she would be faced with a thousand tiny decisions, and each one would either lead her back into the darkness or toward the light of life.

I reminded her that she didn't get where she was

overnight. It took thousands of tiny decisions to get there, and it would take thousands of tiny decisions to get out. But each day as she took tiny steps toward the light, she would move slowly to-

ward a brand-new life. I promised her that one day, after thousands of tiny steps in the right direction, she would wake up surrounded by the light of God. Months later she wrote me a note telling me how marvelously her life has changed in the last ten months. She lives and walks in the light of God's love every day. It is nothing short of a miracle.

We only make progress when we walk in the right direction. To use the words of 1 John 1:7, we must actively choose on a moment-by-moment basis to "walk in the light."

Some missionaries who share Christ with hardcore gang members in Chicago asked me to do a radio interview with several former gang members who have been reached for Christ through their ministry. I was delighted to say yes. As we drove to the studios, I listened as the three young men shared how they met Jesus Christ. These guys had done it all and seen it all. They spoke about the life they had lived before Christ and about how He had miraculously transformed them, giving them a brand-new direction. They are on fire for Jesus.

One of the young men I met was the eighteen-year-old leader of a group of gang members who have committed their lives to Jesus Christ and are now trying to influence their friends. He said that just one day earlier someone had approached him and asked if he wanted to help cut and sell $10,000 of cocaine. The man would put up the money if the young man would help sell it on the street. The young man said he could easily sell that much in a month or two and clear

$50,000. When I asked him how much he could make in a year selling drugs, he paused and thought about it. Conservatively, he could make $200,000, but $300,000 wouldn't be out of the question.

That young man has experienced more of life in eighteen years than most people see in eighty years. But when he met Jesus Christ, his life was radically transformed. When I met him, he was studying to be an electronics specialist. He's praying for a Christian wife and for the chance to raise a family for the Lord. He's also thinking about the ministry.

So when the offer came to sell cocaine, he said no. That's all. He just said no. Sure, the money looked good, and he knew exactly how to make a huge profit. But he didn't have to pray about it. He just said no.

Sometimes we make spiritual growth more difficult than it is. If you want to make progress, you've got to start taking tiny steps in a new direction. You have to say no to sin and yes to God. You have to do it hundreds and even thousands of times each day.

Most of us won't get hit with the proverbial lightning bolt that radically changes us overnight. But by God's grace we can be changed little by little. By God's grace, we'll move forward in simple faith, taking one tiny step at a time.

Before we know it, the sunlight will come flooding in, and we'll wake up to discover that we are walking with Jesus Christ, in the light of His love, and He is walking beside us.

Lord Jesus,
You have set me free
from sin and its
dreadful penalty.
Help me today to walk
in the light, that I
might have fellowship
with You. Amen

Name a few small daily decisions that have a huge impact on whether you walk in light or in darkness.

Think about the changes Jesus has made in your life. Spend time thanking Him for His grace to you.

What small steps toward the light do you need to take this week?

How to Walk on Water

Matthew 14 : 29 b

Then Peter got down out of the

boat, walked on the water

and came toward Jesus.

I know a man who walked on water. It doesn't seem possible, but it's true, and it happened like this. Jesus is on the northwestern shore of the Sea of Galilee. It is late in the day, and He has miraculously fed five thousand people with a few loaves and a handful of fish. After dismissing the crowd, He sends the disciples ahead to the other side of the lake, telling them He will meet them later.

That night a massive storm blows across the lake. For hours the disciples struggle to keep the boat afloat. Sometime between 3 A.M. and 6 A.M. Jesus begins walking on the water. I don't know how He did it, but *that* He did it I have no doubt. After all, He is the Lord of earth and heaven, the Lord of the natural and the supernatural. Walking on water would not be difficult for the Son of God.

When the disciples see Him walking on the water, they are terrified. They think it is a ghost. I cannot blame them a bit. My first thought would *not* be, "Well, here comes Jesus. He's decided to walk on the water in the middle of this storm." I think I'd be one of the fellows saying, "Shut up and keep rowing."

"But Jesus immediately said to them: 'Take courage! It is I. Don't be afraid.' 'Lord, if it's you,'

Peter replied, 'tell me to come to you on the water.'
'Come,' he said" (Matthew 14:27–29).

---

*When Jesus says, "Come,"
you'd better obey. When He
says, "Walk," you'd better walk.
Once Jesus gave the command,
the safest thing Peter can
do is to get out of the boat.*

It's a rule of the spiritual life that when Jesus says,
"Come," you'd better obey. When He says, "Walk,"
you'd better walk. When He says, "Come toward
me," you'd better come toward Him. Once Jesus
gives the command, the safest thing Peter can do is
get out of the boat.

As Peter starts walking toward Jesus, a mighty wind

begins blowing across the lake. For an instant, he forgets about Jesus and remembers who he is and where he is. He is Peter, a Galilean fisherman who belongs back in the boat. He looks down at his feet and sees nothing but water underneath. His mind comes to a quick conclusion: "I'm not supposed to be walking on water. This is impossible."

Before we go any farther, let's analyze that thought. From one point of view, Peter was correct. From the human perspective, what Peter was doing was impossible. Walking on water is contrary to all known laws of science. It contradicts scientific theory and the history of human experience. You might call it the Second Law of Hydrodynamics: *people don't walk on water.* In all of human history, no one (except Jesus) had ever walked on water before. So you can hardly blame Peter for coming to that conclusion.

~

There is only one thing wrong with this logic. Peter was walking on water. Therefore, it couldn't be impossible. Unlikely, yes. So rare as to be unheard of, yes. But impossible? No. Walking on water was not impossible, because Peter himself was doing it.

~

Peter hardly has time to think it through logically. He sees the wind blowing, he panics, and in that split second, he comes to the wrong conclusion. That's when he begins to sink. Peter shouts, "Lord, save me" as he is going under. The Bible says immediately Jesus reaches out His hand and catches him. That means Jesus caught him as he was going under.

Jesus' words to Peter are important. "You of little faith, why did you doubt?" (Matthew 14:31). In our English version, "You of little faith" comes out to four words. But in the Greek, Jesus only uses one word—"Little-faith." It's a title or a nickname. Jesus calls Peter "Little-Faith." "'Little-faith,' why did you doubt?"

We live in a world that encourages us to stay in the boat. The message we hear over and over is, "Play it safe. Be careful. Don't take any chances." When our children learn to walk, what do we say to them? "Be careful." The result is a generation of passive young people who don't know how to deal with the world as it is.

If you decide to get out of the boat, you may not be completely successful. Maybe things will work out for you, maybe they won't. If you decide to become a risk taker for Jesus Christ, will you see success in all that you do? Probably not.

Most of the men and women in the Bible who took great risks saw only partial success for their efforts:

- ∽ Abraham made it to the Promised Land but lived his whole life in tents.
- ∽ Moses led his people to the Jordan River but could go no farther.
- ∽ Joshua conquered the land but did not defeat all the enemies.

So it goes for those who live by faith. Our calling is to find out what God is doing in the world, and to fling ourselves wholeheartedly into His cause. If we win, we win. If we lose, we lose. In the end the only real losers will be those who held themselves back.

Where is Jesus today? He's not in the boat. He's out on the water. And He's saying to His children, "You've been in the boat too long. You've been gripped with fear too long. Just keep your eyes on Me, 'Little-Faith,' get out of the boat and come to Me."

In the end, who looks better? Peter who tried and sank, or the eleven who didn't even try? There's a reason we don't preach about the other eleven. They played it safe. Only Peter took the risk. That's why we're still talking about him after two thousand years.

It's risky to walk on water. You might sink. But you'll never know until you get out of the boat.

Heavenly Father, Grant that we might be great risk takers for the kingdom of God. Shake us loose from the security of staying in the boat. Help us to walk on the waters of faith because we believe Jesus will hold us up. Amen

If you had been Peter, would you have gotten out of the boat? Why or why not?

How do we balance the challenge of living by faith with the need to act prudently?

Name a few biblical characters who got out of the boat for God. What happened to them? What inspiration do you draw from their examples?

Unarmed
Faith

1 Samuel 17:40

Then he took his staff in his hand, chose five

smooth stones from the stream, put them in the

pouch of his shepherd's bag and, with his

sling in his hand, approached the Philistine.

L et me give you the best definition of faith I've ever heard: Faith is belief plus unbelief—and acting on the belief part. We all know you have to believe something before you can have faith. If you go to a doctor, you must *believe* he can help you. If you don't *believe*, you'll never go in the first place. Before you step into an elevator, you've got to *believe* it will hold you up. If you don't *believe*, you'll end up taking the stairs. So belief is the first part of faith, the conviction that certain things are true.

Some people stop their definition of faith there. They think faith is belief plus nothing else, pure belief without any mixture of doubt. That's okay as long as you stay in your house, in your bed, under the covers. But in this world, it's hard to arrive at one hundred percent certainty about anything. You *hope* the doctor can help you, but maybe he's a quack. You *hope* the elevator will hold you up, but maybe the cable has gone bad. People who believe faith means one hundred percent certainty are paralyzed. They are waiting for something that will never happen.

In truth, unbelief is always mixed with our belief. You see it best in big decisions. You get a good job offer in another part of the country. It's a great opportunity, but you don't want to move. You are stuck in your present job, but the kids are happy in school. Your wife doesn't want to move, but you've found twice the house for half the money. You think you should, but some of your friends aren't sure. Late at night you lie awake tossing and turning, first going one way, then another.

That's reality. You don't have one hundred percent certainty, and you don't know any way to get it. You think, you hope, you pray for guidance, you seek counsel, you write it all down, you wait for a lightning bolt from heaven, but it never comes.

What is faith? In the big decisions of life, faith is *not* waiting for 100-percent certainty. Faith is wavering between belief and unbelief, doubt and assurance, hope and despair, and finally *acting on the belief part*. Many people think "living by faith" means staying in the "belief" column until you get certainty. But that seldom happens. That's not "living by faith"; That's "stalling by faith." Living by faith means taking a step of faith, however small, however halting, however unsure of yourself you may be.

Most of us know the story of David and Goliath and how the mighty Philistine giant was toppled by one smooth stone. It is an amazing story of faith. Naked faith. Unarmed faith. Faith plus nothing and minus nothing. Faith in God's power in the face of impossible odds.

This truth comes into focus if we ask what might seem like an obvious question: At what point did Goliath die? When did David kill him? You say, "Easy. When he cut off his head." No, not really. "When the stone hit him." No, not even then. Go back a little bit. Was it when he picked up the five smooth stones? No. Was it when he told Goliath what he was going to do? No, but you're close. Was it when he refused to wear Saul's armor? No, but you've passed over it.

Between those two events something critical happened. First Samuel 17:40 tells us after David picked up the five stones, he "approached the Philistine." When he took that first step, Goliath was a dead man. He just didn't know it yet. David won the victory with that first step. The rest is history. David possessed Goliath's head while it was still attached to Goliath's shoulders. Goliath never had a chance. He was just a paper giant.

Did David know something the other men of Israel didn't know? No. They also knew God was great and mighty and powerful. They knew He was the Lord of Hosts. Any one of them could have killed Goliath if they had been willing to take that first step in the name of the Lord. The difference between David and the other soldiers was not that he had faith and they had doubts. Or that they had doubts, while he had none. The difference is this: David acted on his belief and ignored his doubts, while they acted on their doubts and ignored their belief.

Faith is not waiting until all your doubts are gone. If you wait for that, you'll wait forever. Faith is seeing the giant, understanding the odds, believing God wants him dead, and taking that first step. If you can do that, the rest is easy.

Now apply this truth to your life. What giants stand

Faith is wavering between
belief and unbelief, doubt
and assurance, hope and
despair, and finally
acting on the belief part.

in your way today? Name them. Write them down.

Think about how the giants of circumstance and op-

position have combined to keep you enslaved to fear

and sometimes have driven you to the brink of despair.

How much longer will you hide in fear? When are

you going to step into the valley and face the giant

eyeball to eyeball? There are always a thousand rea-

sons to run away when Goliath stands before you.

But whenever you are tired of running, the Lord stands ready to walk into the valley with you.

Sooner or later you've got to peek over the top of the ridge, look into the valley, and take that first step forward. It won't be easy, but you'll never know until you step forward by faith. You take that first step not because you think you can do it but because you know you can't. You know if the giant is defeated, it is because God has done it through you.

*Father, I pray to be
filled with such
confidence in You that
the giants will seem like
grasshoppers to me.
Help me remember
that because You are
big, the problems of
life are small. Amen*

Is doubt always wrong? Why is unbelief (in some form or another) involved in true biblical faith?

Write down a few giants in your life. Ask God to help you to face them head-on.

Read Hebrews 11, and circle phrases that illustrate what it means to act on belief.

Risky
Obedience

Mark 1 0 : 2 9 – 3 0

"I tell you the truth," Jesus replied, "no one who has left home or
brothers or sisters or mother or father or children or fields for me and
the gospel will fail to receive a hundred times as much in this present age (homes, brothers, sisters, mothers, children and fields—
and with them, persecutions) and in the age to come, eternal life."

I received a message from friends who are medical missionaries in an underdeveloped country. They spoke of sickness, danger, lack of medical equipment, and the potential danger to their children of being raised in that environment. After listing some of the problems, they came to the point:

As a parent, it raises lots of concerns—what if it happened to our family, especially our children? Are we ready to handle the fact that our medical resources are limited here? For example, we have one ventilator—used about once a year—that probably wouldn't work well for a child. There is no MRI scan machine in the country, and maybe no working CT scanner. On a smaller scale, the episodes of stomach upset

*and diarrhea are a recurring annoyance, as is
the constant exposure to malaria. Why take the
risk of living here?*

*Perhaps some people enjoy the "thrill" of
such adventures, or risk-taking. If you know us,
you know we don't fit that category! Rather, the
risks we take by living here are part of the risks
we take by believing in that which is not seen—
that is, by believing in God. Placing our faith in
an unseen God IS risky—especially if that faith
demands trusting God's providence in real, tan-
gible ways. Yes, we would prefer to be living
somewhere where a few of the risks were reduced.
But obedience to God at this time in our lives re-
quires that we be in this "risky" environment.*

Ponder that last sentence. They have conclud-
ed that obeying God means they will have to
leave the "safety" of America for the "danger"

of a distant land. They are willing to risk it all to obey God.

Many years ago I heard Vernon Grounds say that whenever you face a major decision, you should ask, "What difference will this make in 10,000 years?"

That helps us differentiate between what matters and what doesn't. Most decisions we agonize over won't matter in three years, much less ten thousand. What will matter ten thousand years from now is whether or not you commit yourself to being God's man or God's woman without reservation, no strings attached.

James Dobson tells of a missionary who came home after a career overseas. He had passed up the opportunity for a lucrative career in the States to serve in the islands of the Pacific. Did

~

Rest easy, child of God. There's a steady hand at the helm, and He doesn't need any help from you.

~

he regret giving up a promising career? As a young man he had wrestled with that. Then one day he went to the church sanctuary, knelt at the altar, and determined to stay there until the matter was settled. Finally he sensed the Lord saying to him, "Sign a blank piece of paper and give it to Me." The man did that, and the Lord said,

"Now let Me fill in the details." Everything that

had happened since then, he said, was God filling in the details.

What is keeping you from obeying God? Where is the "moral" paralysis in your own life? What is God calling you to do that you are resisting? Do you see where your resistance is hurting you?

A friend says he envisions his life as a great ship with the Lord at the helm. Every so often he wants to tap God on the shoulder and say, "Are You sure You know what You're doing?" We all feel that way at times. Rest easy, child of God. There's a steady hand at the helm, and He doesn't need any help from you. But you'll never know until you give Him full control of your life.

❧

Lord of All, Help me to place myself under Your care, holding nothing back, making no excuses, but giving You all things in advance, and letting You fill in the details. Amen

❧

Read Mark 10:29-30 aloud, slowly and thoughtfully. What has it cost you to follow Jesus? What have you gained? Are these words of Jesus true or not?

What does the term "moral paralysis" mean?

What is keeping you from obeying God?

A Sit-Down Salvation

H e b r e w s   1 0 : 1 1 – 1 2

Day after day every priest stands and performs his religious duties; again and again he offers the same sacrifices, which can never take away sins. But when this priest had offered for all time one sacrifice for sins, he sat down at the right hand of God.

I t is difficult for us to grasp these verses because twenty centuries later we live in a different world. Hebrews was written to another group of people, in another time, in another culture. The original readers were Jewish Christians who had been raised in the synagogue, who understood the tabernacle, and knew about the temple in Jerusalem. They were well versed in the Law of Moses, and they knew about the sacrifices and offering. Things that to us are strange relics of the past were to them everyday realities. The passage of time has made it hard for us to understand how revolutionary these words in Hebrews 10 are.

He says "day after day" and "again and again" every priest offers the same sacrifices. The Old Testament specified a variety of offerings, including the burnt offering, the drink offering, and the meat offering. Each offering was performed according to an elaborate, prescribed ritual. The routine of the men who were priests in the Old Testament was a routine of sacrifice and offering, offering and sacrifice—one after the other, morning, noon and night, day in and day out, week in and week out, month in and month out, year after year, decade after decade, century after century.

During the 1500 years from the time of Moses to the time of Christ, hundreds of thousands (if not millions) of lambs, goats, and bulls were offered on the altar before God to make atonement for the sins of the people.

What do we know about the priests? In Hebrews 10:11 we're told every priest "stands" to make his offering.

If you read Exodus and Leviticus, you will find a description of the architecture of the ancient tabernacle. There is detail concerning the coverings of the rings and poles, the brazen altar, the showbread, the candlesticks, the veil, and the furniture inside the Holy Place. But you will never find a description of a chair. There were no chairs in the tabernacle, because the priests were never finished with the work of making sacrifices and offerings before God.

Not only that, we are told those sacrifices could never take away sin. The Greek word in Hebrews 10:11 for *take away* means to strip off. It pictures a tight-fitting sports uniform soaked in sweat that you have to strip off at the end of the day. It refers to sin that seems to wrap around us. The writer is telling us that though you offered a thousand goats and a thousand bulls and a thousand rams, all the blood of all those animals added together couldn't take away one sin. Not even one.

The priest in the Old Testament had steady employment, because he was always offering sacrifices. He was so busy he could never sit down. He had a job that was guaranteed to bring him nothing but frustration, because every time he made a sacrifice, he had to make another one, and another, and another.

Suppose you were a priest in the Old Testament and

you somehow lived to be 1000 years old. From the day
you were born until the day you died, you offered a
lamb in the morning and a lamb in the evening. You
never missed a day. By the day you died you would
have lived 365,000 days and you would have offered
730,000 lambs to God. Do you know how many sins
you would have forgiven? Not one.

Jesus did what the priests
could never do. One man, with
one offering, paid for sins forever.
He finished it and sat down
at the right hand of God.

The first word in verse 12 is the most important
verse in the book of Hebrews. *But.* Circle it. Under-
line it. Your salvation depends upon that one little

word. You are going to heaven because of that word
but. On one side stand the priests doing the will of
God day after day; week after week, and year after
year—killing the animals, making the sacrifices,
making the offerings before Almighty God. Their
hands are stained with blood. When one of them dies
another one steps up to continue.

*O*n the other side stands one man. His name is
Jesus Christ. Between the priests of the Old Testament and Jesus Christ there is the little word
but. That *but* makes all the difference. Jesus did
what the priests could never do. He sat down be-

cause His work was finished. One man, with one offering, paid for sins forever. He finished it and sat down at the right hand of God.

❧

Do you know the difference between religion and Christianity? It's two letters versus four letters. Religion is spelled with two letters—D-O. Religion is a list of things people think they have to *do* in order to be accepted by God—go to church, give money, keep the Ten Commandments, live a good life, be baptized, pray every day. The list is endless. It's always Do . . . Do . . . Do. Most people believe if you want to go to heaven, you've got to *do* something and keep on doing it until the day you die.

❧

Christianity is spelled with four letters— D-O-N-E. Christianity is not based on what we *do* but upon what Jesus Christ has *done*. If you want to go to heaven, you don't have to *do* anything; you just have to trust in what Jesus Christ has *done* for you.

Do versus *Done*. Either you *do* it or you believe that Jesus Christ has already *done* it for you. Which is it for you?

Lord Jesus,
I praise You that
the work of salvation
is complete. When
You said, "It is
finished," You meant
it. Hallelujah!
Amen

Why did the Old Testament priests stand while performing their duties? Why is Christ now seated at the right hand of God?

Read Hebrews 10:1-14. Why is it impossible for the blood of bulls and goats to forgive sin?

In your own words explain the difference between religion and Christianity.

By Faith Alone

Romans 3:28

For we maintain that a man is

justified by faith apart from

observing the law.

The word *justify* means "to declare righteous." The term comes from the courtroom of the first century. As a trial drew to a close, the judge, having heard all the evidence, would pronounce his verdict. To justify a person meant to declare them not guilty in the eyes of the law.

There is another way to understand the term. If you have a computer, you probably know what it means to have justified margins. A justified margin is one that is straight from top to bottom. The computer arranges the words and spaces so all lines end the same distance from the end of the page. In that sense, *justify* means "to make straight that which would otherwise be crooked."

Take those two concepts together. When you trust Jesus Christ as Savior, God declares you "not guilty" of sin and "straight" instead of "crooked" in His eyes. It is an act entirely performed by God on the basis of Jesus' death on the cross. We receive it through faith alone. Nothing you do—nothing you ever could do—contributes to your justification. It is an act of God on the sinner's behalf.

The crooked is declared straight and the guilty sinner is declared righteous in God's eyes. Until you understand this, you could hardly claim to understand the gospel. Luther called it "the cornerstone of Christianity." Justification is the doctrine that answers the question, "How can a person be made right with God?"

Why can't good works save us?

First, good works can't cancel your sin, but sin ruins your good works. Suppose you invite me over for breakfast and offer to fix a three-egg omelet. As you begin to cook, I smell a putrid odor coming from the kitchen. What's that awful smell? It's just a rotten egg. But you added a few good eggs to cancel out the rottenness. Do you think I would eat your omelet? Not for a million dollars. Because goodness doesn't cancel rottenness, but rottenness ruins goodness. The same is true in the spiritual realm. You can't be good enough to cancel out the putrid effect of your sins.

Second, good works can't save you because God doesn't grade on a curve. He demands perfection. It only takes one sin to send you to hell. Let's suppose you somehow committed only three sins a day for your entire life. That's impossible for most of us because we commit that many sins before getting out of bed in the morning. But let's give you credit for being good. That would be more than one thousand sins a year, which would mean that in seventy years you would end up with over seventy thousand sins on your record. If those sins were speeding tickets, you'd end up in jail so long they would throw away the key. Do you think God is any different?

Our sins are like a mountain—so high we can't climb over it, so wide we can't walk around it, so deep we can't tunnel under it. Our sins are so great our works could never save us.

Third, good works can't save you because you can never be good enough, long enough. Just when you get a "good streak" going, you sin and have to start all over again.

When you trust Jesus Christ
as Savior, God declares
you "not guilty" of sin and
"straight" instead of "crooked"
in His eyes. It is an act
entirely performed by God
on the basis of Jesus' death
on the cross. We receive
it through faith alone.

Fourth, you can never be sure you've done enough. Religious people have no assurance of their salvation.

They believe being good will get them to heaven. But as we've already seen, we can never do enough to pay for our own sins.

Finally, good works can't save you because if they could, you wouldn't need Jesus. Why would Jesus die on the cross if you could save yourself? When we get to heaven, no one will be able to say, "You and me, Jesus, we did it together." It's either all by Jesus or all by your own efforts—there's nothing in between.

How, then, are we saved? If not by our own good works, how will we get to heaven? If not by our righteousness, where will we find the righteousness we need?

During the Reformation, John Calvin and Martin Luther said we are saved by the application of an "alien righteousness." To most of us the word *alien* conjures up visions of strange little creatures with no hair and bulging eyes. But that's not what Luther and Calvin meant at all. The word *alien* simply means "from another place."

To say we are saved by an alien righteousness means we are saved by righteousness that comes "from another place." It comes not from within us as a result of our good deeds, but from outside us entirely. Where can a guilty sinner find righteousness from another place? In Jesus Christ. That's the alien righteousness that saves guilty sinners. Salvation is outside you and me. We do not save ourselves; we contribute nothing to our salvation—nothing at all. God calls us, His Spirit draws, He gives us faith to believe, and He applies to us righteousness from another place—the righteousness of His Son, Jesus Christ.

This means there is nothing you can do to add to the work of Christ. It stands complete on its own. You either accept it or reject it.

Where do you stand with God today? Are you straight with Him or is your life still one big crooked mess? Have you been justified by faith alone?

*Righteous Father, I bless
You that my salvation
does not rest on what I
do or how I feel but on
what Christ has done for
me. I bless You for the free
gift of righteousness that
is mine through faith
in Him. Amen*

Why do we need to be justified? Why can't we save ourselves by good works?

What is alien righteousness, where can we find it, and why do we need it to reach heaven?

What happens when we try to add anything to the work of Jesus Christ on our behalf?

Faith for Your Children

H e b r e w s   1 1 : 2 0

By faith Isaac blessed Jacob and Esau in regard to their future.

Genesis does not give us much information about Isaac. He is overshadowed by his father, his wife, and his two sons. Isaac is manipulated by his wife and both his sons, and he seems helpless to stop the scheming. He has a strong father, a protective mother, and a domineering wife. He never steps out of the shadows and establishes his own identity.

Yet the Bible says, "By faith Isaac!" He must have done something right. At what point do we see his faith in action? We see it when Jacob puts on the goatskins (at his mother's instruction) and fools Isaac into thinking that he (Jacob) is his hairy brother Esau. Isaac then gives Jacob the blessing he intended to give to Esau. Later when Esau asks his father for a blessing, the deceit is discovered. This is the crucial moment. Isaac knows he has been tricked into giving Jacob the blessing. Everything about the way it was done was underhanded and wrong. Yet Isaac refused to reverse what he had done. "I blessed him—and indeed he will be blessed" (Genesis 27:33). Later he gives Esau a blessing, but it is less significant.

Isaac didn't try to reverse the blessing obtained through deceit, because he believed God was at work even in the trickery of his wife and his younger son. He affirmed God's choice of Jacob over Esau and God's blessing of Jacob though he did not deserve it. By faith he ratified what God ordained. What a lesson this is about the sovereignty of God working through sinful human circumstances. Isaac understood God's will comes first, and we must bow before it even when we don't understand it.

Sometimes we make decisions that hurt those we love the most. When that happens, we must do what is right even when it goes against our personal preferences. At that point will we put God's will above our own desires?

Did Isaac have faith? Yes. He was strong in the end when it counted. He made sure his children were blessed. He didn't accomplish a great deal from a worldly point of view, but he passed his faith along to his children. In the end, that's what matters.

I find myself challenged by this fact. If I gain the world but lose my family, my life can hardly be called a success. If I lose the world but save my family for God, my life will not have been in vain.

When you die, the most important thing you leave behind will be your Christian faith. The people of my congregation will know me better after I am gone. When we live close to others, we may find it difficult to get them clearly in focus, but when they are gone, we can take the full measure of who they were and what they lived for. Those who know me will know what I believed and how I lived by watching my sons and my grandsons and granddaughters after I am gone. They will tell the story for me. They will rise up and reveal what sort of man I was. Both my strengths and weaknesses will be easy to see. If they live for Christ, all else will fade away. If they don't, nothing else can suffice.

This is not to say we can control how our children

will respond to the gospel. We all know children have minds of their own. After all, Isaac and Ishmael went different ways, as did Jacob and Esau. I know of no way to guarantee that your children will share your faith in Jesus Christ. One may go to the far country of sin while the other stays home and faithfully fulfills his responsibility. And when the prodigal returns, the child who stayed home may feel resentful. Life is like that sometimes.

The great evangelist Billy Sunday is buried not far from my home. Almost every year I portray him in a "cemetery walk" sponsored by our local historical society. He preached to 100 million people face-to-face and saw more than one million "walk the sawdust trail" to shake his hand and claim Jesus as Lord and Savior. Billy and his wife, Helen "Ma" Sunday, are buried side by side, with their three sons nearby. Ironically all three sons disappointed him and often shamed him by their sinful behavior, which was wide-ly publicized during his lifetime. This fact cannot can-cel his enormous achievements as an evangelist, but it does point out that great success in the ministry does not guarantee success at home.

Isaac didn't accomplish
a great deal from a
worldly point of view,
but he passed his faith
along to his children.
In the end, that's
what matters.

Abraham was hardly perfect (he lied about Sarah be-ing his wife—not once, but twice). Isaac had many flaws (he lied about his wife, Rebekah). Jacob was a born cheater and had problems with his brothers. Joseph wasn't a cheater, but his brothers couldn't stand him at first. And so it goes. All these men—flawed as they were—lived and died by faith. Their children followed them both in their strengths and in their weaknesses, and ultimately in their faith. God uses imperfect people, because that's all He has to work with. The perfect people have all gone to heaven.

Ruth Bell Graham says a saint is a person who makes it easy to believe in Jesus. If our children follow us in our faith, we can die happy knowing we succeeded in the one place it really mattered.

Spirit of the
Living God,
Fill me with Jesus
so when others
follow me
they are really
following Him.
Amen

Read Genesis 25-28. What was Isaac like? What were his strong points? His weak points?

If you have children, what are your dreams for them? If you could ask God for one thing for each of your children, what would it be?

What can you do to make it easy for others to believe in Jesus?

Faith for Your Grandchildren

Hebrews 11:21

By faith Jacob, when he was dying, blessed each of Joseph's sons, and worshiped as he leaned on the top of his staff.

Jacob is now an old man. One by one he calls in his sons and gives each one a blessing suited to him. When he comes to Joseph, he blesses him and then he blesses Joseph's sons Ephraim and Manasseh.

The story of the blessing of the grandsons is interesting, because Jacob did an unexpected thing. Joseph wanted him to bless Manasseh the older with his right hand as a sign of the greater blessing. But at the last second Jacob crossed his hands and blessed Ephraim the younger with his right hand. This displeased Joseph, but Jacob would not change his blessing. Some of us who are younger sons and daughters can draw great encouragement from this story. Many times the firstborn children are favored and children that come later are overlooked. But the Bible is full of hope for younger children. Isaac was a younger child. So was Jacob. So was Joseph. So was Moses. So was Gideon. So was David. In blessing the younger over the older, Jacob teaches us that God exalts those who honor Him regardless of their background or birth order. Often through the "overlooked" people of the world, God does His greatest work.

Jacob knew his grandsons Ephraim and Manasseh

had been raised in Egypt's luxury. Because of Joseph's exalted position, they had been reared to appreciate all that the pagan world had to offer and to enjoy all the glories of ancient Egypt. But Jacob looked into the future and saw a day when his descendants would return to Canaan. He wanted to make sure his grandsons embraced their spiritual heritage.

If you stay in Egypt, you cannot be blessed. You must leave Egypt for the Promised Land. By blessing his grandsons, he was moving them from worldly pomp to godly poverty. He did it "by faith" because he judged that God would keep His word and that the ragged tents of Canaan were a greater treasure than the vaunted temples of Egypt.

Jacob's faith was strong as he came to the end of life. How could he be filled with such confidence? After all, he was a schemer, a cheater, a compulsive manipulator. All his life he had worked the angles to get ahead. Years earlier he had deceived his father and cheated his brother.

With such a checkered past, how could he be so joyful? The answer goes to the heart of the gospel. In the words of R. T. Kendall, God held him guilty for nothing. I do not doubt that during the long years when he thought Joseph was dead, Jacob felt guilty and probably thought Joseph's fate was his fault. If only he had been a better father. If only he had provided stronger leadership. If only, if only, if only. But in the end it didn't matter. All of God's purposes fit together.

~

Jacob worshiped with joy as he thought of the happy ending of a life filled with sadness, anger, betrayal, separation, loneliness, and manipulation. Jacob couldn't undo his mistakes. But he rejoiced in the end because he knew God had forgiven him. As he looked into the faces of his beloved grandsons, he could see God had orchestrated every detail.

~

God exalts those who
honor Him regardless
of their background or
birth order. Often through
the "overlooked" people
of the world, God does
His greatest work.

~

In this there is hope for every sinner. God takes our wicked past and places it on His Son, Jesus. God works through our sinful choices to accomplish His divine plan. This doesn't make sin any less sinful, but it does demonstrate God's glory in overcoming evil with good.

Recently I spoke with a man who has gone through many years of personal and marital difficulty. The last time I had seen him—many months earlier—his face was taut and his voice filled with anger. He seemed about to burst wide open with rage. But now his countenance shines with peace and joy. What happened? God had to bring him to the end of his rope and let him hit rock bottom. It was humbling and frightening. But as he told me the story, he emphatically declared: "It had to happen this way. I see that clearly now." Everything had to happen exactly as it did so God could work a miracle in his life.

Now he and his wife get up every morning at 5:30 to read the Bible and pray together. Because I know the man well, I can say it is a miracle—only God could have done it. It is a great advance in faith to look back over years of pain and foolish decisions (by yourself and by others) and be able to say, "It had to happen this way."

When you can see God's hand even in the mistakes of life, when you can smile with joy as you consider what God has done for you, you have discovered the same faith Jacob had.

*Father, When I am
confused and downcast by
my circumstances, remind
me that nothing happens by
chance. Grant me faith not
to give up when I feel like
quitting. I bless You because
Your love endures to a
thousand generations. Amen*

"If you stay in Egypt, you cannot be blessed." What does
Egypt represent for you?

What does it mean to say, "God held him guilty for nothing"? How can that be possible?

Pray for each member of your family by name.

Faith for the Distant Future

Hebrews 11:22

By faith Joseph, when his end was near,

spoke about the exodus of the Israelites from

Egypt and gave instructions about his bones

M ost of us know Joseph's story (Genesis 37-50). His brothers envied him. They sold him to the Midianites, who took him to Egypt where Potiphar purchased him as a slave. Later he was falsely accused by Potiphar's wife and thrown into prison. Finally, as a reward for correctly interpreting Pharaoh's dream, he became second in command in Egypt. His family in Canaan thought he was dead, but through extraordinary events eventually they discovered the truth. The family moved to Egypt where they enjoyed a happy existence for many years. Joseph saw God's hand in everything that had happened to him, telling them, "You intended to harm me, but God intended it for good" (Genesis 50:20). A few verses later we find his last recorded words:

"I am about to die. But God will surely
come to your aid and take you up out of this land
to the land he promised on oath to Abraham,
Isaac and Jacob." And Joseph made the sons of
Israel swear an oath and said, "God will surely
come to your aid, and then you must carry my
bones up from this place" (Genesis 50:24-25).

Though he was dying, Joseph knew that God would keep His promise to deliver the Israelites from Egypt and give them a homeland of their own. Because he believed, he instructed the Israelites not to leave his bones in Egypt but to carry his mummified body with them and give him a burial place in the Promised Land.

How could he be so sure? He knew what God had promised his great-grandfather Abraham (Genesis 12:1-3). His own life proved God keeps His promises. He knew Israel didn't belong in Egypt, and he didn't want his bones staying in Egypt when the Jews left for Canaan. On the outside he looked like an Egyptian; on the inside he was an Israelite.

The Bible tell us Moses took the bones of Joseph with him when the Jews left Egypt (Exodus 13:19) and Joshua buried them at Shechem (Joshua 24:32).

It is worth pausing to consider what this means.

Joseph's great-grandfather died and was buried in Canaan. His grandfather died and was buried in Canaan. He had seen to it that when his father Jacob died, his remains were taken from Egypt and buried in the cave of Machpelah near Mamre (Genesis 50:1-14). From Abraham to Isaac to Jacob to Joseph, the tradition passed on: bury me in the Promised Land.

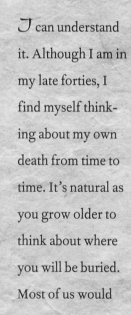

I can understand it. Although I am in my late forties, I find myself thinking about my own death from time to time. It's natural as you grow older to think about where you will be buried. Most of us would like to be buried near our loved ones, if possible. We want our final resting place to be a testimony that we belong somewhere, that we didn't just live and die by ourselves, but we came from a family. That's why in most cemeteries you see family plots with a mother and a father buried together, and children (often grandchildren, too) buried nearby. Those plots bear testimony to the power of family ties to overcome the pain of hurt feelings, misunderstandings, harsh words, and years of separation. They proclaim to the world, "We were together in life, and we are together in death."

Several years ago, on the first day of our family vacation, we made our way south from Chicago, heading down to Mississippi and on to Florida. We were having a great time, singing, laughing, and telling jokes. We stopped for lunch in southern Illinois, got back in the car, and headed down the road. We hadn't gone far when our resident theologian Mark (who was then ten years old), asked me, "Dad, when you die, where do you want to be buried?" How do you answer that? I replied, "In the ground." But Mark was serious, so we discussed the question for a few minutes. It was important to him to know the answer.

❧

Joseph knew that God would keep His promise to deliver the Israelites from Egypt and give them a homeland of their own.

❧

Joseph lived and died without hearing about Moses and Joshua. He knew nothing of their mighty deeds. But in his old age God gave him faith to believe that although he was dying in Egypt, his future belonged in the Promised Land. Joseph was saying, "I may be dying, but I believe one day God will keep His promises. I want to be there when it happens so don't leave me down here in Egypt. Bury me in the Promised Land."

When a man or woman of God dies, the promises of God live on. They bury us, but they don't bury God's promises with us. Your death cannot nullify God's faithfulness. Our God is the God of the future. He is the God of the generations to come.

A servant whose master was dying was asked, "How is your master?" "He is dying full of life," came the reply. It is a grand thing to die full of life. This is possible for those who know Jesus Christ as Lord and Savior.

*Lord God, I praise
You that death cannot
cancel Your promises.
Grant that when this life
is over, I may still be
with You, in Your
presence, beholding
Your face, for all
eternity. Amen*

Why was it important for Joseph not to be buried in Egypt?
How can your burial site be a testimony to your faith in God?

Have you ever known a person who died full of life? How is
that possible?

What Bible passages give you hope as you think about the
prospect of your own death?

Faith That
Gives God Glory

O swald Chambers said, "Faith is deliberate confidence in the character of God whose ways you may not understand at the time."

N ot long ago I preached on the story of Nebuchadnezzar losing his mind and becoming like a beast of the field for seven years (Daniel 4). It all started when the king had a dream of a vast tree with branches stretching out in all directions and birds of every kind coming to nest in the branches. Suddenly the tree was cut down and the stump was bound with iron and bronze. The good part comes at the end when the king's sanity is restored, his reign is increased, and he openly gives God glory for all that had happened.

The story teaches us how God deals with His children. Sometimes He shakes our tree to get our attention; sometimes He cuts the tree down. He never does either to hurt us, but rather to strip away our excessive self-confidence and bring us closer to Him.

A few days after I preached on Nebuchadnezzar's story, a friend sent me a note that said:

I want to thank you for your prayers and for the sermon. I found it most applicable. Now I have an image to work with. Last year was definitely the tree-shaking time, and now I am little more than a stump. That's exactly how I feel. But how encouraging to know that from here, through the awesomeness of God, He will raise me up to be a tree again. And I pray a wholly submissive one.

My sister said something cool that she kept reminding herself last year when going through a difficult time: "It's okay to be the queen who reigns in the Land of Uncertainty for a time, because you know your Father is the King of the Land of All-Knowing."

I don't know where she came up with that, but it fits. Well, it will be an interesting year and probably a tough one, but with God in control, an awesome one.

Faith believes when it cannot see and trusts God when nothing seems to make sense. If your tree is shaking, or if you hear "Timber!" in the distance, don't despair. God loves to turn stumps into beautiful trees once again.

About the Author

RAY PRITCHARD (Th.M., Dallas Theological Seminary; D.Min., Talbot School of Theology) is senior pastor of Calvary Memorial Church, Oak Park, Illinois, where he lives with his wife and their three children. He is the author of *Keep Believing; Green Pastures, Quiet Waters; The ABCs of Wisdom; Something New Under the Sun;* and *An Anchor for the Soul.*

Moody Press, a ministry of Moody Bible Institute, is designed for education, evangelization, and edification. If we may assist you in knowing more about Christ and the Christian life, please write us without obligation: Moody Press, c/o MLM, Chicago, Illinois 60610.